The HOPE HANDBOOK

POWERFUL, INSPIRATIONAL, HOPEFUL TWEETS THAT ENCOURAGE MOTIVATE, AND SPEAK TO YOUR SPIRIT

THE SEARCH FOR PERSONAL GROWTH

GERMANY KENT

STARSTONE

The Hope Handbook

Copyright @2015 by Germany Kent

Visit us on the Web at www.TheHopeHandbook.com

ISBN: 978-0-9961468-6-9 (ebook)
ISBN: 978-0-9961468-7-6

Library of Congress Control Number: 2015903590

Compiled by Germany Kent

Published by: Star Stone Press, 10736 Jefferson Blvd #164, Culver City, CA 90230

Printed in the United States of America

Amongst inspirational tweets of hope compiled using wise words from my grandmother, original content, and tweets of knowledge from other tweeters, you will find words of hope passed along from many other wise people who have crossed my path on my journey to self-discovery. You will also find motivational messages as spoken or written by world leaders and motivational gurus.

Books are available in quantity for promotional or premium use. Requests for information should be addressed to: Star Stone Press, 10736 Jefferson Blvd #164, Culver City, CA 90230, for information and discounts and terms. You may also send a request at www.GermanyKent.com

CONTENTS

REFLECTIONS
MEDITATIONS
INSPIRATIONS

"Every choice we make literally is a seed that we sow, and every seed that we sow will bring some kind of harvest in our life."

–Joyce Meyer

INTRODUCTION

Your world is shaped by the power of your words and how you use those words to motivate yourself. Life is about having clarity and joyful thoughts that lead to personal growth, productivity and prosperity. Your thoughts get richer with the positive input you deposit into your spirit. Unfortunately, not every day is a good day. I get that. There are even a few days of bad luck that linger and make it difficult for us to focus and see our purpose. You must remember that you are not stuck, only in transition. The truth is, walking in your purpose and having passion makes the cup almost always seem half full.

We all want to feel happy and hopeful all the time, and we're fascinated by others who seem to be. How do they do it? How can we do it, too? Sometimes we're faced with BIG decisions on our journey that may require us to reevaluate where we are, and in what direction we are headed. At times like these, it is important to go deep within yourself in search of your higher calling. I refer to this as our search for personal growth.

Is there hope? Yes. It is possible to be completely fulfilled in life.

Understand that hope begets hope. The more uplifting and encouraging words you inhale, the more positive you become. Don't you agree? Personal growth in life is directly related to what we think about and the types of messages we receive into our spirit. Therefore, you are what you read.

This book is a place to start. Here's what you'll find between the covers: perspective, inspiration, insight, rules of the game, and focus points to help you commit to set new achievable objectives leading you to greater happiness and prosperity.

A hopeful mindset is what will set you apart from your competitors. I know, because I've practiced it year after year. I only got it right when I took the time to observe what successful people do. In short, they don't sweat the small stuff and they work continuously on themselves. That knowledge I now happily pass on to you.

No matter how you read this book, you'll find it's jammed with good advice, great ideas, important reminders, and words of hope to carry you through your day, week, month and the rest of your life.

You'll come away knowing that your outlook on life is directly related to what you deposit in your soul. There is a mission residing in you waiting for you to walk into your purpose. The good news is, by reading this book you're winning because you're taking the right steps toward having a brighter future!

"If you don't like where you are,
move on. You're not a tree."

PART ONE

SOW SEEDS OF HOPE

"Judge each day not by the harvest you reap,
but by the seeds you plant."

Robert Stevenson

🐦 The first person who needs to believe in you is you!

🐦 When you realize that every word spoken has great impact you'll craft every sentence to generate life and create lasting legacy.

🐦 Each time you open your mouth you inform others of your state of mind and the condition of your heart.

🐦 Not looking back is the hardest part about moving forward.

🐦 Dreams do turn into reality. Some take time. Some take hard work. Some take collaborations. Keep your dream alive. It can come true.

🐦 Hope means intentionally using the idea of a future to keep you from experiencing the present. It's a crutch, but if you feel lame, use it.

🐦 Be happy not because everything is good, but because you can see the good side of everything.

🐦 Be hopeful. Be around hopeful people. Personify hope. Give hope.

🐦 You can't have a positive life with a negative mind.

🐦 Someone's inability to recognize your value and appreciate your brilliance is a problem on their end, not yours.

🐦 Once you replace negative thoughts with positive ones, you will start having positive results.

🐦 The world is full of nice people. If you can't find one, be one.

🐦 The difference between impossible and possible is a willing heart.

🐦 Never let someone's opinion of you become your reality.

🐦 Today you can refuse to think negative thoughts, speak negative words, or engage in any negative behavior.

🐦 Sometimes you have to encourage yourself with the same advice you give to others. Praise yourself for all the lemons you've turned into lemonade.

🐦 Surround yourself with those who see greatness in you, even when you don't see it in yourself.

🐦 Today will never come again. Be a blessing. Be a friend. Encourage someone. Let your words heal, not wound.

🐦 Free your mind from negativity.

🐦 Be careful who and what you allow to deposit into your spirit. What you take in will definitely shape what you put out.

🐦 Misery loves company. Happiness doesn't need it.

🐦 The strongest people are not those who show strength in front of us, but those who win battles we know nothing about.

🐦 It's amazing what happens when you just won't give up.

🐦 Life is about learning, growing, giving, sharing, and loving ourselves into a state of unconditional, peaceful acceptance.

🐦 Believe that good things will happen, and they will.

🐦 There is too much negativity in the world. Do your best to make sure you aren't contributing to it.

🐦 Be somebody who makes everybody feel like a somebody.

🐦 Let your spirit of excellence be contagious.

🐦 If plan A fails, remember there are 25 more letters.

🐦 Just smiling more can cure your misery.

🐦 "B positive" is not just a blood type, but a way of life.

🐦 Life is not just about the destination, but about our journey and the people we touch along the way.

🐦 Sometimes the things we retweet speak louder than what we say.

🐦 Speak it until you believe it and believe it until you see it!

🐦 Let there be peace on earth, and let it begin with me.

🐦 Your biggest obstacle is worrying about tomorrow. Today needs you more.

🐦 Positive minds produce positive lives.

🐦 Be kind. Be a friend. Be a hero. Be you. Be happy. Be grateful. Be here now. Be a warrior. Be an inspiration. Be inspired.

When your mind says give up, hope whispers one more try.

Live without pretending, love without depending, listen without defending, and speak without offending.

🐦 Until you wholeheartedly believe in your own value, worth, and worthiness, there will always be a void in your spirit.

🐦 Alter your attitude and you can alter your life!

🐦 Accept the exceptional value in you.

🐦 You have to believe in affirmations before they work.

🐦 Nobody's a natural. You work hard to get good and then you work hard-er to get better.

🐦 A kind heart and compassion are the real sources of peace and happiness.

🐦 Call the things you desire into being so that your life will come into alignment with your greatest expectations.

🐦 The difference between an opportunity and an obstacle is your attitude.

🐦 You are never too old to set another goal or to dream a new dream.

🐦 Every time you feel discouraged, close your eyes and visualize the future you want. Then open your eyes and start building until you get there.

🐦 What you put out to the universe always comes back to you. You have a choice to exude great vibes everyday.

🐦 Feed your dreams and starve your fears.

🐦 Remember how far you've come, not just how far you have to go. You are not where you want to be, but neither are you where you used to be.

🐦 Never give up. Always find a reason to keep trying.

🐦 Expanding your mind is expanding your reality.

🐦 To change culture, change character. To change character, change consciousness of character in daily decisions.

🐦 Speak those things that are not as though they were; your confessions to yourself are how you make claims on what is to be!

🐦 Love and Positivity will change the energy around you to create a more positive mindset. Remember your thoughts and actions = your reality!

🐦 Elevate your mind to think GLOBAL, not LOCAL.

🐦 Be...here...now! You are already the person you aspire to be, now if you only believe and train your thoughts you will amaze yourself.

🐦 Life: Forgiveness, Random acts of kindness, giving back, and courage to move forward.

🐦 Accept what is. Let go of what was. Have faith in what will be.

🐦 Just because you can't see it yet, doesn't mean it's not on its way.

🐦 Your focus should be how many revenue streams you can create with your talent, who you can impact, not necessarily where you are today.

🐦 Upgrade your life by prioritizing more and sitting around less. Get up, get out, and DO something. Don't let the days of your life pass you by!

🐦 You cannot find peace by avoiding life.

Happiness is a choice. Optimism is a choice. Kindness is a choice. Giving is a choice. Respect is a choice.

Never underestimate the power you hold within, for everyone has an untapped source deep within their soul.

🐦 Talking about our problems is our greatest addiction. Break the habit. Talk about your joys.

🐦 When we feel like a bird with a broken wing, we won't know we've healed if we don't try to fly again and keep trying until we fly confidently.

What we think will come out of our mouths, actions and attitude. Think things that add to your life, not things that draw away from your life.

A healthy attitude is contagious but don't wait to catch it from others. Be a carrier!

🐦 A positive attitude gives you power over your circumstances instead of your circumstances having power over you.

🐦 People who change the world start by changing themselves.

🐦 Always keep an open mind and an open heart, and the solution you seek will come your way.

PART TWO
BLOOM WHERE
YOU'RE PLANTED

"Always do your best. What you plant now,
you will harvest later."
Og Mandino

🐦 Don't be a detrimental host to your own exponential growth.

🐦 Everyone is capable of taking his or her life in a new direction.

🐦 You'll never get "there" if you keep standing "here." There is not here.

🐦 The world is only as limited as your mind.

🐦 Want to get unstuck? Stop blaming others and assume full responsibility for your life.

🐦 The only way to get to where you want to be is to do what needs to be done to get there.

🐦 Don't expect to see a change if you don't make one.

🐦 Champions are not the people who never fail, but the people who never quit.

🐦 You attract the right things when you have a sense of who you are.

🐦 If you want to achieve greatness stop asking for permission.

🐦 Most people who are successful have done more than study the successes of others. At some point, you have to get up and do the work yourself.

🐦 Don't be afraid of change. You might lose something, but you may gain something better.

🐦 You must begin to think of yourself as becoming the person you want to be.

🐦 Stop letting others define you. Stop letting others dilute you. Don't be bullied or pressured into being less than you are.

🐦 Don't spend your life trying to impress other people. Do what *you* love, love what *you* do.

🐦 Imagine all the things you could do if you were not afraid.

🐦 The only way you lose is if you give up.

🐦 You were born to journey in the direction of your purpose. Anything that halts your progress is contrary to your design.

🐦 Miracles never happen without movement. If you are expecting a miracle move to it don't just sit there.

🐦 If you wait until you're ready, you'll be waiting the rest of your life.

🐦 Life doesn't get easier or more forgiving; we get stronger and more resilient.

🐦 Enjoy the skin you're in...it only fits you!

🐦 Your lack of motivation is what's stopping you, not somebody else.

🐦 Don't be afraid of being different. Be afraid of being the same as everyone else.

🐦 No matter how you feel, get up, dress up, show up, and never give up.

🐦 The first step towards getting somewhere is to decide that you are not going to stay where you are.

🐦 If you wish to fly, then you must give up the things that weigh you down!

🐦 Don't make excuses. Excuses give you permission to remain where you are.

Your future is not ahead of you, it is trapped within you. Release your future and manifest your destiny.

It's actually easier to change the uncomfortable parts of your life than it is to keep on perpetuating a negative cycle.

🐦 Nobody can make you happy until you're happy with yourself first.

🐦 The flower that blooms in adversity, is the most rare and beautiful of all.

🐦 Nothing works unless you do!

🐦 Life's biggest limitations are the ones you make in your own mind.

🐦 Believe in yourself.

🐦 Study yourself.

🐦 You become a person of influence by first becoming a person of purpose.

🐦 We don't mature through age; we mature in awareness.

🐦 When you stop chasing the wrong things, you give the right things a chance to catch you.

🐦 When someone tells you it can't be done, it's more a reflection of their limitations, not yours.

🐦 If you don't try, you'll never know.

🐦 The world will be a better place when the power of love replaces the love of power.

🐦 Walk in your purpose.

🐦 If you have a hard time achieving your goals, change your strategy.

🐦 You can't have a good day with a bad attitude, and you can't have a bad day with a good attitude.

🐦 Why compare yourself with others? No one in the entire world can do a better job of being you than you. Be the best version of you.

🐦 The future is not ours to see, but it is ours to create.

🐦 Everybody has a talent, but it's what you do with it that makes it great.

🐦 Greatness is upon you.

🐦 Do what makes you happy, be with who makes you smile, laugh as much as you breathe, and love as long as you live!

🐦 Every person, situation, circumstance, and experience in your life is a reflection of some aspect of who you believe yourself to be.

🐦 It takes clarity to flow in divine authority.

🐦 You cannot always change your situation but you can accept your assignment in that situation.

🐦 When you've got something to prove, there's nothing greater than a challenge.

🐦 Your attitude and outlook on life are 100% your responsibility.

🐦 Growth begins at the end of your comfort zone.

🐦 The only way to grow to another level is to pass through the corridor of discomfort.

🐦 To champions, failure is a temporary setback, not a defining moment.

🐦 The worst thing you can do is ruin your potential by staying comfortable.

🐦 You are not responsible for the emotions of others. We all have to master our own state of mind.

🐦 Living things grow. Are you still growing?

🐦 Never be ashamed of being you because in your uniqueness lies your purpose and special gift to the world.

🐦 Every accomplishment starts with the decision to try.

🐦 You can't please everyone. The best thing you can do is believe in yourself and do what you think is right for you.

Do not limit your challenges; instead challenge your limits.

You must train your mind to look for the good in all. Only then will you learn to break down barriers that divide.

🐦 Don't be too hard on yourself. It takes time to actually change after you understand how to.

🐦 Stop knocking on closed doors and new doors will open.

🐦 Think deeply, speak gently, love much, laugh often, work passionately, give freely, and be kind.

🐦 Follow your hunger for knowledge. New appetites form new aptitudes to solve problems that lead to promotion!

🐦 Decide what you want, believe you can have it, believe you deserve it, believe it's possible for you.

🐦 Crush your fears. Soar to new heights. Believe the unbelievable.

🐦 The only person who is truly holding you back is you. No more excuses, it's time to change. It's time to live life at a new level.

🐦 Do something today that keeps you connected to your inspiration.

🐦 Your destiny is in your hands. Creating the life you want is only and always up to you.

PART THREE
ENHANCE YOUR GRATEFUL GARDEN

"Your mind is the garden, your thoughts are the seeds,
the harvest can either be flowers or weeds."

William Wordsworth

🐦 Give thanks for unknown blessings already
on their way.

🐦 A good life is when you assume nothing,
do more, need less, smile often, dream big,
laugh a lot, and realize how blessed you
are.

🐦 Loving yourself means that you accept responsibility for your own development, growth and happiness.

🐦 Life is a miracle. Stop focusing on the negative. Instead focus on the flower inside that blooms with self-love.

🐦 Life is full of give and take. Give thanks and take nothing for granted.

🐦 Being kind to others always increases you. Being mean to others always diminishes you.

Never let the things you want make you forget the things you have.

Be mentally attractive.

🐦 Choose to feel blessed. Choose to feel grateful. Choose to be excited. Choose to be thankful. Choose to be happy.

🐦 Kindness costs nothing, yet one day, you may need the favor returned. Then it will mean everything.

The condition of your heart will determine what you see. If the condition of your heart isn't good you can be in a good place and not see it.

If you want to feel rich just count all the blessings you have that money can't buy.

You cannot be inspired if you are surrounded with negativity. Open the door and step into the inspirational garden of nature.

Don't confuse your value with your valuables.

🐦 People will sooner see the value in you,
when you first see the value in yourself.

🐦 You can't be jealous of someone else's
results. You don't know the prayer,
process, sacrifices, and work they endured
for it.

🐦 F.L.Y. - First Love Yourself.

🐦 You are a work in progress, a seed growing into a flower.

🐦 Be a part of something bigger than yourself.

🐦 Find a balance between contentment and ambition. Learn to enjoy where you are on the way to where you are going.

🐦 Peace of mind requires keeping your mind on the right things.

🐦 Maybe if we spend just a little time saying "thank you" for what we do have, we won't have time to dwell on what we lack.

🐦 Be thankful for today, because in one second, your entire life could change.

🐦 Some people can have all the lights on and still be in the dark.

🐦 There is always something to be thankful for.

🐦 Attract what you expect. Reflect what you desire. Become what you respect. Mirror what you admire.

🐦 The minute that we think that we know it all is the moment that we have stunted our growth! There is always more to learn...

🐦 Listen more. Observe more. Understand more. Strive for more. Love more. Give more. Be more. Learn more. Forgive more. Live more.

🐦 Never allow a bad day to make you feel like you have a bad life.

🐦 Life is so unpredictable that it causes an exhilarating vigor for actually living.

🐦 If the biggest thing we do in life is extend love and kindness to even one other human being, we have changed the world for the better.

🐦 The only thing that makes life unfair is the delusion that it should be fair.

🐦 The worst person to be around is one who complains about everything and appreciates nothing.

🐦 It takes a second to think before you act, but a lifetime to fix the mistakes of not taking that second.

🐦 You were born with your own GPS. It's called your intuition. Trust it. Use it.

🐦 You give power to the things you choose to focus on so choose wisely.

🐦 Find peace within yourself.

🐦 We forget that happiness doesn't come as a result of getting something we don't have, but by recognizing and appreciating what we do have.

🐦 Gratitude turns what we have into enough.

🐦 If it doesn't agree with your spirit then let it go.

Blessed are those that can give without remembering and receive without forgetting.

The sign of a beautiful person is that they always see beauty in others.

Be strong enough to stand alone, smart enough to know when you need help, and brave enough to ask for it.

It costs $0.00 to be a nice person, so stop acting like you can't afford a good attitude.

🐦 Stop focusing on what's wrong with everyone else and start focusing on how blessed you are!

🐦 Sadness steals your smile. Anger steals your laughter. Hate steals your heart.

🐦 Every flower has to grow through dirt.

🐦 Don't ever say "I want what they have!" you never know what they went through to get it. You need to walk in your own purpose.

🐦 How you do anything is how you do everything.

🐦 It doesn't matter how someone else acts. What matters is that you know what you believe and you live your life accordingly.

If our hours are filled with regrets of yesterday and the worries of tomorrow, we have no today in which to be thankful.

Life is not having and getting, but rather being and becoming.

- Determine what in your life brings you happiness and make sure to focus some time each day on those activities.

- Whatever problem you're experiencing someone else is experiencing or has gone through it. If they made it, so will you.

🐦 It's important to make someone happy and it's more important to start with yourself.

🐦 Change the way you see things and things you see will change.

🐦 Focus on your goals, not your problems.

🐦 If we expect more grace we must be more humble. The greater amount we need, the more humble we should become. Pride is met with resistance.

When you make a difference in someone's life you make a difference in all the lives they touch.

Don't let your limitations overshadow your talents.

🐦 You are enough. You are so enough it's unbelievable how enough you are.

🐦 Not all wounds are so obvious. Walk gently in the lives of others.

🐦 The power of a positive mind is priceless...

🐦 Stop majoring in the minor stuff.

If we prepare our minds and hearts for victory then we can't be consumed with fear and doubt.

Life is what you make it so be careful with what you create.

🐦 Always be kinder than necessary. How you treat others reflects your true character.

🐦 The sun will rise whether you are prepared to enjoy it or not.

🐦 Do not struggle against the current of life. Go with it without resistance and be open to seeing the blessings along your way.

🐦 Accept no one's definition of your life; define yourself.

🐦 Happiness will never come to those who fail to appreciate what they already have.

🐦 The people you think you can't learn something from are the main people you can learn from.

🐦 Speak in such a way that others love to listen to you. Listen in such a way that others love to speak to you.

🐦 Don't live the same day over and over and say it's a life. That's surviving. Living is growing, improving, learning, evolving, changing.

🐦 Things money can't buy:

1. Manners
2. Morals
3. Respect
4. Character
5. Common sense
6. Trust
7. Patience
8. Class
9. Integrity
10. Love

PART FOUR
NEW SEASONS
OF INCREASE

"You must take personal responsibility. You
cannot change the circumstances, the seasons,
or the wind, but you can change yourself.
That is something you have charge of."

Jim Rohn

🐦 BREAKING NEWS: Today is a new day. Don't get stuck in your yesterdays.

🐦 Old doors close because new doors are opening.

🐦 Let go of the "what was" and "what could have been" and focus on the "what is" and "what can be."

🐦 Respect yourself enough to walk away from anything that no longer grows you.

🐦 Decide not to let old habits rob you of new beginnings.

🐦 Chaos is letting go: letting go of people, emotions, and things that threaten to destroy us, thoughts that sabotage us, and memories that prevent us from moving forward.

Adversity awakens a determination in those who passionately commit to continue moving forward regardless of what stands in their way.

Don't talk about what you want, be fearless enough to get it!

🐦 Every trial we face is a new opportunity to grow.

🐦 Define success on your own terms, achieve it by your own rules, and build a life you're proud to live.

🐦 Engage, Enlighten, Encourage and especially...just be yourself! Social media is a community effort, everyone is an asset.

🐦 Focus on where you are going instead of being obsessed with where you have been.

🐦 Sometimes, your circle decreases in size, but increases in value.

🐦 Be the peace this world needs, be the love this world lacks, be the difference, be the change, be the revolution.

🐦 You can't reach what's in front of you until you let go of what's behind you.

🐦 Problems are like washing machines: they twist us, spin us, and knock us around, but in the end we come out cleaner, brighter, and better.

🐦 The sky isn't the limit; the mind that sees the sky is the limit.

🐦 Every moment in life is a chance for a new beginning.

🐦 Surround yourself with people who will speak life, but tell you the truth.

🐦 Stop bringing yourself down or selling yourself short so that others can be comfortable with who you are.

🐦 Happiness will come to you when it comes from you. Success will be yours when you choose to take responsibility for making it so.

🐦 Sometimes out of our greatest rejection comes our greatest direction.

🐦 Dust yourself off and get back in the race.

🐦 If you want to regain the momentum you lost, wind up and take off down the path of prosperity and growth.

🐦 Life is not just about achievement. It's about learning, growing, and developing qualities like compassion, love and joy.

🐦 If you continue to do the same thing, you will continue to produce the same results. Try something new!

🐦 You cannot create great things until you believe you were created to create great things - believe in your greatness.

🐦 If you believe it will work out, you'll see opportunities. If you believe it won't, you'll see obstacles.

🐦 Sometimes you just have to die a little inside to be reborn again as stronger and wiser version of yourself.

🐦 Avoid unnecessary complexity, as tempting as it becomes.

🐦 Don't let your failures define you. Let them refine you into a more humble, dedicated, faithful and passionate person.

🐦 A good day is a good day. A bad day is a good story. At the end of the day it's all good.

🐦 You'll meet two kind of people in your life: ones who'll build you up and ones who'll tear you down. In the end, you'll thank them both.

🐦 Moving forward is not the same thing as moving on. Forgive, disconnect and move on.

🐦 If you had never tasted a bad apple, you would not appreciate a good apple. You have to experience life to understand life.

🐦 You can't have a poverty mindset with trump dreams!

🐦 You know you are on the right track when you become uninterested in looking back.

🐦 There are some people who are attached to you while others are actually assigned to you. It's important to know the difference!

🐦 We cannot rush the sunrise or pay to bring on the full moon. Everything will happen when it's supposed to happen.

🐦 Don't cry over the past. It's gone. Don't stress about the future. It hasn't arrived. Live in the present and make it count.

🐦 What defines us is how well we rise after falling.

🐦 If it's meant for you to have it, you'll get it; If it's not, you won't, and you're no less if you don't.

Don't regret yesterday; it is the perfect compass guiding your journey today.

Every day presents a new opportunity to make new memories.

🐦 It takes "lacking" to appreciate more, cold to know warmth, absence to appreciate presence. Every place has a purpose.

🐦 When you focus on being the best person you can be, you draw the best possible love, life, and opportunities toward you.

🐦 Quality is never an accident; it is always the result of high intention, sincere effort, intelligent direction, and skillful execution.

🐦 Most people only exist. To live is a rarity.

🐦 Do not talk about the way you are; talk about the way you want to be. Direct your future with the power of your words.

🐦 A time will come when dreams meet reality. This is the time your life begins, when destiny unfolds before you.

🐦 Be driven with purpose and relentless in your alignment with excellence.

🐦 Life is what you make it. We do not fail. We succeed in finding out what does not work.

🐦 Insecure people who lack vision see strong people as competition. Secure people with vision see them as partners and wonder how they can build together?

🐦 You were born to win, although to be a winner, you must plan to win, you must prepare to win, you must expect to win.

A positive attitude brings much gratitude! Think positive, be positive, speak positive and stay positive.

Difficulties come into our lives to develop us: every storm is a school, every trial is a teacher, every experience is an education.

🐦 There is no one path to success, there's no big break...the big break is a series of smaller successes which culminate into one big moment!

🐦 If you are ready to shape your destiny, change your life, and be more fulfilled, then you have to embrace change.

🐦 Don't miss the magic of the moment by focusing on what's to come.

🐦 There are no secrets to success. Success is the result of preparation, hard work, and learning from failure.

🐦 Keep charging ahead and don't take no for an answer. Expect miraculous solutions to appear.

🐦 Good things come to those who believe, better things come to those who are patient, and the best things come to those who don't give up.

New doors open when you're ready to walk through them. Once you're in a place where you're truly prepared for it, the portal becomes visible.

Massive action is the key to all success.

🐦 Until you wholeheartedly believe in your own value, worth, and worthiness, there will always be a void in your spirit.

🐦 Sometimes we need to be hurt in order to grow. We must lose in order to gain. Sometimes lessons are learned best through pain.

Opportunities are out there waiting for every smart person to snatch them.

You cannot change what you will not confront. Confrontation leads to transformation!

🐦 Don't live the same day over and over and say that's a life. That's surviving. Living is growing, improving, learning, evolving, changing...

🐦 How we interpret a situation determines how we experience it. You can create new experiences by thinking differently about what you encounter.

The secret of happiness, is learning to embrace your unhappy thoughts with love, by shining light on your darkness.

Work your hardest. Think your smartest. Dream your biggest. Be your greatest. Love your fullest. Smile your brightest.

🐦 Everything in your life is a reflection of a choice you have made. If you want a different result, make a different choice.

🐦 At times life does not seem to recognize or reward our efforts but if we maintain our efforts reward is inevitable.

🐦 Your smile is your logo. Your personality is your business card, how you leave others feeling after having an experience with you becomes your trademark.

🐦 Laugh. Dance in the rain. Cherish the memories. Ignore the pain, love and learn, forget and forgive, because you only have one life to live.

A beautiful life does not just happen. It is built by daily prayer, humility, dedication, and hard work.

I fall, I rise, I make mistakes, I live,
I learn, I've been hurt but I'm alive.
I'm human, I'm not perfect, but I'm thankful.

ONE DAY AT A TIME

H.O.P.E: Have Only Positive Expectations

ACKNOWLEDGMENTS

My gratitude goes to the many motivational gurus who have inspired me throughout my life with their powerful written words intended to bring about personal growth. Thank you for sharing your insight and wisdom. At a very early period in my life, I became attracted to self-help personal growth books. I don't remember a time when I didn't have a book of inspirational quotes as my companion. I'm a huge fan of motivation — especially self-motivation!

Since learning is experiential, and most often life lessons learned are through trial-and-error, I was able to bounce back quickly from defeats and setbacks knowing that someone else had made it through what I was experiencing. That gave me hope to try again and taught me to be resilient and courageous enough to keep going. There have been times when these motivational guides offered much peace, and hope. I'm a better person today because of you and I wish to pay tribute to all of those authors who have come before me with words of hope, inspiration, and motivation!

Finally, I would like to mention the affection of those around me, especially my followers on Twitter, who have supported me all along the way, retweeting and providing favorites, replies and mentions to my tweets. Thank you. I am overjoyed!

I write to provide support, warmth, and a voice of hope on Twitter. I hope you have found strength through the messages conveyed in my tweets. Compiling this book has been such a blessing. May you find something valuable within these pages that inspire you to take more risks in your own life, walk in your purpose, and reach greater heights. I wish all of you a road ahead that brings fulfillment, balance, abundance, and a gratifying future. God bless you.

ABOUT THE AUTHOR

With more than a decade of experience, **Germany Kent**, also known as The Hope Guru™, has enjoyed a successful consulting/coaching business with clients from all walks of life. Germany is a dynamic public speaker. She has been awarded multiple times for speaking.

She has appeared nationally on The Drs, The Food Network, NBC, CBS, ABC, Disney, MTV, and BET, just to name a few.

She was previously listed in Who's Who Among Young Americans.

As Germany's brand has grown, both domestic and internationally, she has picked up more than a few fans who remain interested in her status. This has catapulted her into a category of respected power and influence, especially on social media, where she has been cited as a top influencer.

Germany is dedicated and committed to giving back to the community. She has been involved with the Red Cross, The United Way, The Salvation Army and many local charities. Her desire to give back and be involved in the community is a direct result of her humble beginnings being a member of a globally impactful organization, her sorority. She also credits her sorority with teaching her how to mentor and help others, another platform that Germany is immensely committed too.

She graduated with honors from The University of Alabama and

Mississippi State University. She resides in Southern California where she is an entertainment host and successful commercial actress. As a media personality, Germany has interviewed power-players, newsmakers and Hollywood royalty. She has landed interviews with Oscar, Emmy, Golden Globe, and Grammy-award winning performers.

Germany offers messages of HOPE on Twitter and continues to be a social media magnet.

You can follow her @germanykent to receive her messages of motivation and inspiration onto your timeline.

TO OUR READERS

Star Stone Press, publishes books on topics ranging from spirituality, personal growth and self-help to inspiration, technology, family, and social titles. Our mission is to publish quality books that will contribute to the wellbeing of the reader.

Our readers are our most important resource, and we value your input and ideas. Please feel free to contact us.

Mail to:

Star Stone Press
10736 Jefferson Blvd #164
Culver City, CA 90230

If you have enjoyed this book, Germany Kent would love to hear from you.

Please contact Germany at:

TheHopeGuru.com

Printed in Great Britain
by Amazon

57472165R00109